UNFORGETTABLE ATLANTA

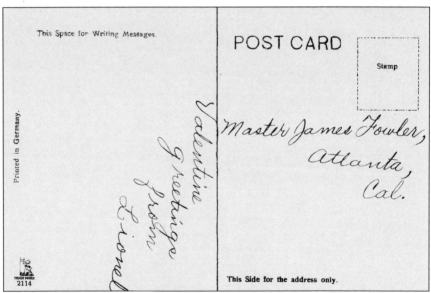

This historical postcard was addressed to "Master James
Fowler, Atlanta, Cal." Courtesy of Marge Fowler Price.

UNFORGETTABLE ATLANTA

by
Elsie Alfieri

RIPON, CALIFORNIA
2002

Produced and designed under the direction of
Arthur H. Clark Company
P.O. Box 14707
Spokane, WA 99214

LIBRARY OF CONGRESS CATALOG CARD NUMBER 2001135865
ISBN-0-87062-314-1

Contents

Illustrations

Foreword

History is so fascinating. Those of us who have lived a long time in an area or district have had the making of history woven into our lives like a living tapestry. Names of pioneers are important marks which embody the definition and consciousness of the existence of those who came before us and of the many unimaginable sacrifices they endured.

If you, the reader, are new to an area, it would certainly enrich your knowledge of where you are just by seeking out the historic past of wherever you settle. You can be carried away on your thoughts as you peruse the local, colorful happenings in histories written by those who lived here before you.

During my high school years, I became interested in knowing more about the Atlanta District located in California's Central Valley where I grew up. The inspiration evolved through friendships with local older pioneers—most of them of Irish descent. It was a fortunate day for me when I had the pleasure to interview the two O'Malley sisters, Margaret and Jane. They were the last surviving children of John and Anne O'Malley. Another old-timer was John Brennan. He and his wife Mintie lived across the street from my family's little farm. He spent hours talking with me about the Atlanta District. I truly regret that the new owners of the O'Malley place razed the lovely old home.

I am looking far back in time—to when the area we now know and refer to as the great Central Valley was a huge lake. Standing on top of Mount Diablo and looking east, one could see water right up to the foothills of the Sierra Nevada Mountains. Today, travelers to Sonora can see the water marks on the sides of those foothills, and notice the gradual reduction of water from its higher level. Due to some seismographic event, the lake drained and the land eventually became a vast desert. Nature beckoned its wildlife to come down from the mountains and forage for food. Deer, elk, bears, many birds, snakes and lizards, to mention a few, came to inhabit this dry, vast stretch of land.

The discovery of gold in the Mother Lode attracted world-wide attention. The Gold Rush brought dreamers, adventurers, immigrants, farmers and others from all walks of life to the northern and central parts of California. Most of the folks were looking for a better life in the new land and some thought their stay would just be long enough to amass a fortune and then return to their homeland. Many, however, came to stay. Settlers found the rich soil of the great Central Valley wonderful for farming, especially after the coming of irrigation. Eventually, agriculture would become the mainstay for the local economy.

It took daring and courage for those early settlers who struggled to settle the land. They must be credited for their tenacity and fortitude in living with and overcoming the formidable situations facing them against all odds in this new land. Look back into local history and read about the pioneers—what they did and how they worked and sacrificed for what they believed would be a better life.

It is my hope that you will find this book informative and interesting. It covers only the area of Atlanta.

ELSIE ALFIERI

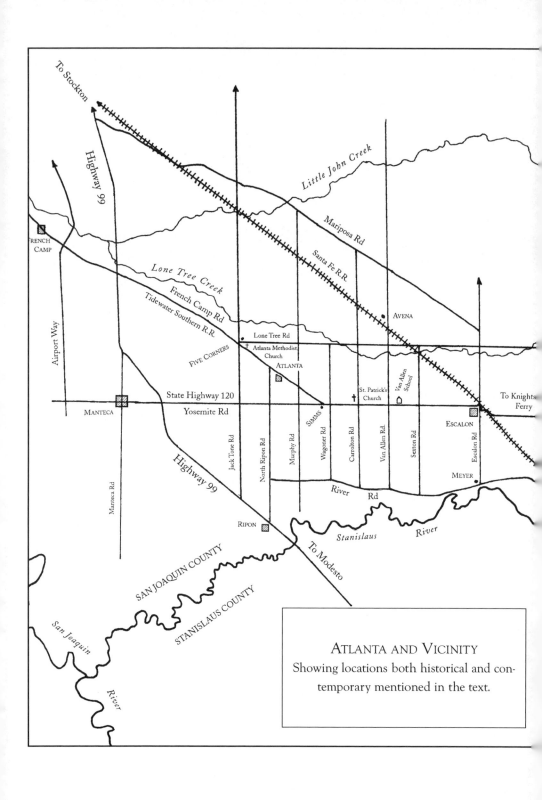

ATLANTA AND VICINITY
Showing locations both historical and contemporary mentioned in the text.

Atlanta

San Joaquin County, California

Fate, it seems, was bent on bringing some special people to settle on barren desert-like land to build a town, so that is how the town of Atlanta came into being. The Atlanta District encompassed a large territory to the easterly line of San Joaquin County and south to the Stanislaus River, and north to the Collegeville settlement. The town itself was established at a spot about a mile or so east of the intersection of Jack Tone Road and French Camp Road, near Due Road. The Due family, pioneers in the Atlanta District, owned land where the road bears their name. In those days, naming a community or town was probably touchy. There are two versions of the origin of the name Atlanta. One version is that Lee Wilson, a native of Atlanta, Georgia, named the town in California for his home city. The other version is that William Dempsey, who was Atlanta, California's, first postmaster, never forgot the kindness and hospitality of Atlanta, Georgia, when he was there as a runaway boy and gave the village the name of Atlanta. Wilson built the first store in the settlement of Atlanta in 1860 and William Dempsey bought it from him in 1860. He named it "The Atlanta Store."

The first post office was established at Atlanta on June 10, 1868, in a corner of a store owned by John D. and

W. L. Murphy. It was known as Murphy Brothers' Store. The name "Atlanta Post Office" was printed in large black letters across the top of the door. Postal records for October, November, and December, 1904, show that $2,163 in postage was sent from Atlanta during those three months. Murphy Brothers Store was destroyed by fire in the 1940s.

Mail for the post office came by train to a station named Ellisworth which later became known as the town of Avena, located about five miles northeast of Atlanta on the east side of Carrolton Road. Before Atlanta grew, a rider on horseback was dispatched to get the mail. A long-time resident of Atlanta, Domenic Nepote, related that later on there was an appointed person who had his own horse and buggy and whose job it was to travel to Avena daily to pick up the mail. This person, I was told, liked his whiskey and by the time he arrived to the depot at Avena, he had passed out in his buggy. The horse knew the way to Avena and when it arrived with the buggy and the unconscious occupant, the station master would toss the bundle of mail into the buggy, turn the horse around, and the animal would return to Atlanta. All the while, the driver would be passed out. Seemingly, there was never any lost mail and the buggy always arrived at the Atlanta post office on time! In those early days there was no mail delivery to homes and businesses as we know it today. People in the area had to travel to the Atlanta Post Office to get their mail. Sometimes, depending where in the wide open spaces one resided, the trip to the post office was quite lengthy.

Other old-timers who were postmasters at Atlanta included Luther Martin (1872); John D. Murphy (1874); John Liesy (March 1886) and W. L. Murphy (November

1886). W. L. Murphy served as postmaster until Mary G. DeHaven took the position in 1914. She continued in that position until the Atlanta Post Office was abandoned in 1915. She was known as postmaster also.

John D. and W. L. Murphy (the Murphy Bros.—as they were known by everyone), also operated a ferry down at the Stanislaus River where the golf links are today. The road which is now called Murphy Road, was for many years know as Murphy's Ferry Road. There were many ferry systems up and down the Stanislaus River as there were no bridges to cross over into Stanislaus County from the San Joaquin County side.

Atlanta was growing given that Manteca, Ripon, and Escalon did not yet exist. Atlanta had a blacksmith shop, wagon shop, saloon, post office and a wagon building shop as well as two churches, one Catholic and one Methodist. The main street of the town was a dusty dirt road which was known as French Camp Road and most of the traffic going to the mines traveled this way. Mariposa Road to the north, originally an Indian trail, was impassable when it rained because the wagons would get stuck in the heavy clay soil. Therefore, travelers learned that the best way to go was through Atlanta on French Camp Road. But, miners and traders soon found out that the more popular place to stop was at the John Jones place near the end of French Camp Road. The Jones family served up great meals which included local game such as bear, deer and many smaller animals. Jones owned a large tract of land in the east end of the Atlanta District. However, Murphy's Store at Atlanta carried all the necessities such as paint, soap, beer, and staples. In the general merchandise area, customers could select gingham, brooms for the school house, axe handles, nails, rope, lamp chimneys, underwear, shirts, shoes, thread, buggy whips, bucksaws, blasting powder, axle grease and stationery. An old ledger dated June 21, 1885 shows prices of some items sold at the Murphy Store as follows: one-quarter pound ground cloves, 15 cents; one thirteen-pound ham, $1.68; small box of soda crackers, 65 cents; one dozen cans of oysters, $1.50; four cans of salmon, 50 cents; five yards of toweling, $1.l0; one pair overalls, 65 cents; one five-gallon can of castor oil, $8.00; one pitchfork, 75 cents; five pounds of sugar, 30 cents; one can of coffee, 50 cents. The coffee was not all real coffee. At the settlement of French Camp, there was a large chicory mill where chicory was dried and processed and shipped off to coffee companies where it was mixed with the real ground coffee beans. The mixture had a somewhat bitter taste and I remember reading on the cans that the ingredients consisted of chicory and ground coffee beans.

In 1912, Atlanta became a stop for the Tidewater Southern Railway which carried passengers in electrically operated coaches. The town became the most important of the 36, or so, passenger stops on the line between Stockton and Modesto. Briefly it was thought there would be a boom and 11 streets were surveyed. However the growth of nearby Manteca and Ripon drew settlers away. Automobile competition plagued the railway passenger service which ceased in 1932. Today, the railroad tracks are still there and are being used by other freight train lines. The town of Atlanta gradually died in the 1920s and L. A. Sprague moved one of the stores west to Simms Station on the railway line. (See "Simms Station")

Cattle raising was a principal occupation and animals just grazed all over as there were no fences. As more settlers came along, eventually vast grain fields were planted, especially in the southeast section of San Joaquin County. Lack of equipment brought about innovations. Of course, we have all heard that "necessity is the mother of invention." Grain farmers would walk the land scattering the grain seed by hand. Then several teams of horses were harnessed and they would drag large branches (from the great number of oak trees in the area) over the seeded ground to cover the seed. Water was not available except in the form of rain. If it rained enough at the right time, the grain would sprout. If the weather did not cooperate, then the crop would be meager. Remember, this was a desert. However, there was so much land planted to grain that the Sperry Flour Company got involved in the area. Also, the Russians sent their emissaries to purchase grain.

The town of Atlanta had some lovely two-story homes. One was the home of Mrs. Mary MacDonald (but note: the name on her gravestone is spelled McDonnell), who taught catechism after school for the Catholic children who attended Atlanta School. I attended Atlanta School for about five months. I loved to go to Mrs. MacDonald's home as she always had a glass of milk and some cookies for us. When it was a warm day, she would have us sit on her big porch for our lesson. Of course after the class, we still had a long distance to walk home. At that time I lived near Simms Station with my family at the home of my uncle, Steve Garibaldi.

The Fisher Stage Line running from Stockton to Sonora stopped at Atlanta for many years and their stages were housed in a barn near Murphy's Store. There the weary horses were unharnessed, stabled, and a fresh team was placed in the traces after which the stage continued its journey.

Sperry Flour Company House
Courtesy of Margaret Carvalho Sciaroni, who was born in this house in the
late 1930s. She grew up with her four sisters and brother here, where her
father and mother also had a dairy.

Atlanta Methodist Church

METHODIST EPISCOPAL CHURCH

In 1878, the Atlanta Methodist Church was erected at a site where French Camp Road and Jack Tone Road intersect. In the late 1880s, the church was regarded not only as a religious center but also as a social center. Early in the 20th century, however, the population was moving elsewhere and the church began to deteriorate. The Atlanta Women's Club was organized in 1928 by Mrs. Albert Due. The club purchased the church building and the land upon which it was situated. Over the years, the club restored the building and made improvements suitable for their use. It was the site of many dinners and dances and other activities which the club actively pursued. The Atlanta Women's Club disbanded in 1998. The building was sold to the Charismatic Community of Evangelization which is under the umbrella of the Roman Catholic Diocese of Stockton.

The land for the Atlanta Methodist Cemetery which lies behind the former Methodist Church was donated by Frederick and Caroline Cook in 1878. This cemetery was originally referred to as the Atlanta Cemetery as it was the only cemetery located in Atlanta. Since the mid–1930s, the Atlanta Women's Club maintained the cemetery. The club made many improvements to the old cemetery which included the erection of a new fence and piping water from the old church building (club house) to the cemetery for the convenience of visitors to the cemetery. Some of the women who were members of the now defunct Atlanta Women's Club are still maintaining the cemetery at this writing.

The flagpole at the cemetery was donated in memory of Leslie and Merlin Miller in 1976.

ATLANTA SCHOOL

The Zinc House School District was formed November 24, 1860 by petitions signed by Patrick Brennan and other early day residents. This petition was approved by the Board of Supervisors. Prior to this time, a small building known as the Zinc House School was used by Earnest Wagoner on his ranch on Wagner Road (formerly Wagoner Road), located just south of French Camp Road which we now know as California State Highway Route 120. The Zinc house served many purposes, but eventually Earnest Wagoner converted it to a school house to educate his children. He hired the son of local pioneers, William Lamasney, as teacher. Later the building was moved near the village of Atlanta and was enlarged to accommodate other children from miles around.

Like other early school districts, Zinc House District took in a large area which was decreased and increased

Atlanta School, 1930s

often by petitions of settlers living on the outer boundaries. For instance, in May 1861 the district was decreased
in size when Wildwood District was started. Increases
were approved in 1865 from Wildwood District and in
1870 and in 1872 from Castle District by recommen-
dation of W. R. Leadbetter who was then San Joaquin
County Superintendent of Schools. In 1874, Gustav
Eichoff and others petitioned to be added to the River
School District. Also, again in 1883, there was a decrease
when Four Tree District was formed from portions of
the surrounding districts. It was the father of May Goodwin Miller, the oldest known living pupil of Zinc House
at that time, together with nine others who petitioned
in 1889 to be added to the Zinc House School District
from Castle District. However, there was another decrease
in 1901 when Calla School District was established. In
1905, H. L. Poynor petitioned to be added to Wildwood
District. Since then, there have been other decreases and
increases in the area necessary to care for the needs of
the people in this and surrounding areas. On November 20, 1915, the Zinc House School District's name was
changed to Atlanta School District by the County Board
of Supervisors after a petition had been presented to them
on November 3, 1915. A new wooden two-room school
building was constructed in 1915 or 1916, and the old
one-room schoolhouse was moved about one-half mile
east by the Murphy Brothers who had been in business
on that site for many years. Later, a stage and auditorium
that could be converted to two classrooms were added.
The last addition of two stucco finished classrooms and
new bathroom facilities was made in 1959 or 1960. Thus,
over the years, the school grew from a one-teacher school
to a four-teacher school, with an instrumental music

instructor for one and one-half days a week. It is interesting to note that two of the early teachers were native born Californians and they were Frank Giles Harriman, born in 1857, and William Lamasney who was born and educated in Stockton. Also noteworthy was the teacher's salary of $85.00 per month in 1885, and of $630.00 per year in 1915. Many descendants of the children enrolled in the 1880s later attended school there and some are still living in the Atlanta area—Carter, Cookson, Due, Miller, Murphy, Foster, Cook, Goodwin, Elenwood and Potter.

On Sunday, December 5, 1971, the Atlanta School was officially closed with a special ceremony at the school in observance of 111 years of serving the Atlanta Community. Mr. Billy Lampkin served as master of ceremonies. The general chairman of the event was Lila Miller. Other Committees were: Sandwiches, Dorothy Elsholz; Cookies, Hilda Lampkin Gibson (Billy's mother); Coffee, Rose Miller and Ann Fisher; Punch, Dorothy Lagier and Mary Rivara; Table Decorations, Carol Ioppini; Publicity and History Seeker, Josephine Hall; Pictures, Althea Mondon; Public Address system, Bill Dias; Flower and table center piece, Jean Due. The committee did a good job and the affair was well attended. Mr. Lampkin said it was sad to close such a good school. Many of the teachers who taught there were mentioned as follows: Irwin Gibbons, Mary Shipley, Estelle Ballati, Norma Ferraiuolo, Patricia Mortensen, Jackie Ballatore, Jane Sandman, Jenny Ramirez, Rudi Richey, Bernice Hall, Lorena O'Brien, Genevieve Ferguson, Frank Harriman, and last but not least, Josephine Hall, who served as teacher and principal for many years. Josephine Hall submitted a brief history of the school and noted that before the schools

came into existence, there was some schooling for children in the area as early education was often privately
financed.

ZINC HOUSE

One could wonder about the name "Zinc House." History tells us that a Mr. E. Allen of Stockton had building materials shipped from New York by way of Cape
Horn at a cost of $1,850. Several writers at the time noted
the coincidence between the freight bill and the year 1850
and wrote—"One dollar for every year that had elapsed
since Christ was born"—quite an observant comment. On
land near Simms Station, Mr. Allen erected his Zinc
House which measured twelve feet wide and sixteen feet
long, with walls seven feet high. This building excited
wonder and admiration. Today it would probably be
referred to as a "pre-fab" building. Its very first use was
as a hotel. The flood of 1852 made travel all but impos-
sible and many of the teamsters spent the winter at the
Zinc House Hotel hoping to find work. That same year,
Earnest Wagoner, a German immigrant, rented the building for five months at the huge rental fee of $800. Sub-
sequently he purchased the property the building was
situated on, and thereby he became the owner of the land
and the Zinc House. His area of property became known
as Zinc House. Many well-guarded stages passed through
the Zinc House carrying Wells Fargo boxes full of money,
gold and other valuables from the mines. Even if a passenger stop was not required, a fresh six horse hitch would
be waiting. Those early-day pit stops to replace tired teams
and hitch up six fresh horses sometimes required less
than two minutes! One stage of the Fisher Lines travelled
from Sonora to Stockton in the latter part of the 1850s

in just six hours, setting a record that was challenged but unmatched for several years. The stage coaches of the Fisher Lines arriving twice daily at the Zinc House were built at Concord, New Hampshire, and cost from $1,200 to $1,500 each. Landscape scenes of California were painted on the outside of the door of each stage. A one-way trip to Sonora from the Atlanta District cost the traveler $16.00. During the Gold Rush, records show that in October 1853, seventy teams were counted daily passing through Wagoner's Zinc House, each team pulling from five to eight tons of supplies going to the mines in the Mother Lode.

Interestingly, it was during that same year, 1853, that the Zinc House Hotel received a future President of the United States as a guest: Ulysses S. Grant came through on his way to Knight's Ferry to visit his sister and brother-in-law, Mr. and Mrs. Dent.

JOSEPHINE HITCHCOCK HALL

An educator bar none, Josephine Hitchcock Hall was someone who told it straight and you knew she meant it. Josephine was a descendant of the Hearty and McCormick families. Those names may not sound familiar to some, but in the past history of "Atlanta" we know that these names were among the names of the approximately eighteen pioneers who gave of their resources and together built the mission church of St. Patrick. They were all well-known folks in the community.

Josephine was born at Atlanta, California, in a home located at the southwest corner of Austin Road and French Camp Road. As of this writing, that home is still standing and in use. She was a lifetime member of St. Patrick's Church.

Those who knew this woman well were aware of her long teaching career in local schools and also the many years she taught at Atlanta Grammar School. Our friend, Antone Raymus told me that she was his 6th grade teacher. He admitted to never studying and to goofing off all the time. One day Mrs. Hall said to him, "you can't go out and play but I will help you with your homework." When they were through, she let him go out and play for the rest of the recess. Because of her determination that he should learn, his grades shot up and he became a good student. Mr. Raymus reflected that she was a wonderful teacher and motivator. He grew up to become a successful realtor and builder of homes in the area.

SIMMS STATION

In the year 1897, Harry L. Simms purchased over two hundred acres from Edward and Myrtle Wagoner and that included land where the sign—SIMMS STATION—still stands today. About 1924, a piece of the property was purchased through a realtor by Mr. and Mrs. Lampkin. They and their young son, Billy, moved into the old Simms home. This home is still standing and in use today. The Lampkins owned all the land up to the confluence of State Highway 120 and French Camp Road. However, during hard times, Mr. Lampkin had to sell off pieces of property, little by little, to make the payments during the Great Depression. About 1985, their son sold the old Simms home and surrounding property to Arvin and Terry Boersma.

Simms Station is still at the same location—where the two aforementioned roads meet. It was, in its heyday, a busy little settlement and the address of folks living there was Atlanta, California. A register showing the names

The repair shop at Simms Station, owned and operated
by Mr. Kreitzer. Courtesy of Escalon Historical Museum.

of the inhabitants of Atlanta showed H. L. Simms as a
resident. When the town of Atlanta died, Merle Sprague
who had a store in town, moved his store to Simms Station on the north side of the road. Later, the store was
sold to Gardner Brothers who operated it for many years.
Eventually they sold the store to Harvey and Fred Peters
and shortly thereafter that historic building burned to
the ground.

Across the road from that store were a gasoline sta-

Sprague's Store. This store was moved from Atlanta to Simms Station when the town of Atlanta was in decline. The building was later sold to Gardner Brothers who operated a general store at that location for many years. The building was sold to Peters in the early 1940s, and subsequently burned to the ground. Courtesy of Escalon Historical Museum.

tion and repair garage, a bar and a blacksmith shop. In 1976, Stockton Production Credit purchased the location and razed whatever buildings were there except for the bar. They hired Roscoe Yater, a contractor from Farmington, to remodel that building. The structure was built of hollow red tile so that was retained. The inside was studded and covered with sheet rock. Mr. Yater informed me that the walls could be 10 to 12 inches thick. At the time of remodeling and making it suitable for an office, a front porch was added for esthetics. The building today houses the satellite office of the San Joaquin County Agriculture Department.

Long, narrow packing sheds lined the railroad tracks on a spur just off the main line of the Tidewater Southern Railroad at the crossing of State Highway 120 at Simms Station. Over the years, much produce, mostly grape, had been packed and shipped from there by rail. Eventually the packing sheds were abandoned and for years were unused. Hoboes passing by sometimes used part of the buildings for shelter or just to sleep out of the weather before moving on. Sometime later, what was left of those packing sheds was razed and not a sign of what was there remains today.

Names of some of the old families or their descendants who still live in the surrounding area include the Fisher family, the Franscella family, Frank and Marge Nunes, and some of the Franzia family members. The Franzia Winery, established by an Italian immigrant, Giuseppe Franzia, is just down the road west on State Highway 120.

The Ripon Fire Station was across the street from the Franscella residence on State Highway 120. That station was moved to a location on Murphy Road. There is a store where Gardner's store used to be and the Fisher home is just east of that store.

In its heyday, Simms Station was also a passenger train stop where the electric cars ran up and down the rails from Stockton to Modesto. One could run out at any spot and flag the passenger cars and the conductor would stop and pick them up. There were, however, designated stations in the Atlanta District and they were: Town of Atlanta, Simms Station, Wagner, Carrolton, Van Allen, Alba, Sexton, Volstead, Escalon, Wigley, and Meyers on the San Joaquin County side of the Stanislaus River. The passenger train traveled on the way to Hilmar in Stanislaus County which was the end of the line.

With the advent of the automobile, the passenger line of the Tidewater Southern Railway was discontinued in 1932. Today, Simms Station is no longer a train stop but it still exists as a landmark.

TWO BRICK BARNS AND WAGONER RANCH

A long barn and grainery were constructed by Earnest Wagoner in 1863 on his land. The bricks for these two large buildings were made on the ranch and the excava-

The two barns built by Earnest Wagoner as they originally stood.

tion site was visible for many years. To get the material to make the bricks, the workers dug down until they came to material called "Madera Clay," six feet below the surface and just below the hardpan. The clay was excavated and a red dye was added to it before the bricks were molded and left to dry. After drying, the bricks were stacked in a kiln where they were baked to a glaze. This process took several days with two crews working to tend the fire in the kiln and remove the bricks. During the course of this project, the crews were served a hot meal at midnight prepared by the Wagoner Family women. After the bricks were finished, work began on the barns. Originally each barn had a storefront reaching to the peak of the roof, but after a severe windstorm, these fronts came toppling down. Although no windows were included in the longer of the two barns, an interesting diamond patterned opening provided light and ventilation. The smaller barn, designed as a grainery, was built to be rodent-proof—that is, without any ventilation whatsoever. By the year 1864, many of the mining claims were declining and travel was becoming less frequent. This situation cut sharply into Mr. Wagoner's business. Always looking for a better opportunity, he made his business into a shipping center for the south county grain farmers. Grain was hauled either to Stockton or to a shipping center, San Joaquin City, on the San Joaquin River (near the Airport Way Crossing) where it was loaded onto barges and shipped to San Francisco. It was no special happening to see forty-mule pack trains pass through Wagoner's place headed for Hornitos, California. Each mule would be carrying two to three hundred pounds of goods including casks of liquor, boxes of tea, bags of potatoes, and bales of dry goods.

The remaining barn as it looks today.

Wagoner built the current house on the ranch in 1910. In 1981, Hazel Woodson, widow of Edward Wagner, (grandson of Earnest Wagoner), had the grainery torn down. Under the floor of the grainery were found many artifacts including some early blacksmith's tools, pieces of china, some Chinese cooking utensils, bottles and other family relics. The bricks from that barn were used to build a home for a member of the Woodson family. The remaining brick barn is one of the last reminders of the Atlanta District's link with the Gold Rush of 1848.

FRENCH CAMP ROAD

French Camp Road began at the settlement of French Camp, so named because of the many Frenchmen who had come to California for the Gold Rush and camped at that location. The road ended at the John Jones residence at a place which would eventually be the location of the town of Escalon. The stage stops of those wild days referred to the road to the Wagoner's Zinc House as the Zinc House Road, but it was really French Camp Road all the time. When the Gold Rush cooled off and business declined drastically, the official name of French Camp Road became more prominent. During the time when the Wagoner stage stop was in full swing, the road ran between the barns and the family home! With the coming of more people and cars and the railroad, the road was finally straightened from Simms Station to Escalon. Today, French Camp Road ends at Simms Station and from thereon it is called State Highway 120 and goes all the way to Yosemite.

AVENA

Avena was big enough to have a post office and the proprietor of a general merchandise store at Avena Station, San Joaquin County, was F. Julius Holm. In October 1897 the first Santa Fe train passed through Avena. This station was among the first to receive shipments of grapes and hay in car lots.

Julius Holm petitioned for a post office at Ellisworth (later to become Avena) and on April 1, 1901, he received

Identity sign as one approaches the town of French Camp (where French Camp Road starts).

the appointment as postmaster. Mr. Holm was from Denmark. In the year 1891 he had come to visit his uncle, Esper H. Due at Atlanta, California. He liked the people and the country and decided to stay. He became an American citizen in 1896.

Avena was an important grain shipping terminal for local grain farmers. Dairy farmers also received shipments of hay for their cattle from this station. Mr. Otto Widman would purchase the hay in Nevada and ship it to Avena. He would then travel by wagon to Avena and pick up his purchase and bring it to his dairy on French Camp Road. Progress in the making! The town of Avena grew rapidly. Already several stores had been lured there from Escalon including a branch of the Irwin Lumber Company from Escalon which was owned by Mr. Sam Irwin, founder of the Escalon State Bank. The bank building in Escalon is still standing at the corner of Main and First streets. As the growth of Avena was rapid, its demise was just as rapid. The post office was discontinued in 1927. Today the only remaining identification of the former town of Avena can be seen as the traveler arrives at the point just before the Santa Fe tracks on Carrolton Road: look to the east where two stately palm trees stand majestically in their abandoned realm and see traces of a once happy home lying in a pile of rubble at their feet. The road passing by is still called Avena Road. It is very still as you pass by and perchance you stop a moment, the faint echo could be hypnotic.

Saint Patrick's Church of Atlanta

The first services of the Catholic denomination in Dent Township were held at the residence of Mr. Carroll in May 1877. Realizing the need for a church building, a subscription was opened resulting so favorably that a committee was appointed and $1800 was subscribed to build a church. Mr. Carroll, John B. O'Malley and B. McMehan formed the committee. The parishioners donated much of the work and St. Patrick's Catholic Church was finished and dedicated in September 1878.

The land for the church and cemetery was donated by John B. O'Malley and the church was dedicated by Joseph Sadoc Alemany, first Archbishop of San Francisco, who was of Spanish descent. Archbishop Alemany's trip from Stockton to St. Patrick's Church was an uneventful one except for the fact that Little John Creek on the way from Stockton was flooded and he had to be carried across. Father W. B. O'Connor of Stockton, at that time pastor of all the Catholic Churches in San Joaquin and Stanislaus Counties, was in charge of the dedication ceremonies.

In the very early years of St. Patrick's there were 150 members of the church with a catechism class of 41 pupils.

Services were held the first Sunday of each month with a priest from Stockton officiating. Sometimes Father O'Connor would remain overnight at the home of John B. O'Malley. The O'Malley family had a special room for visiting priests and bishops in their home. I had a tour of their home when John B. O'Malley's daughters Margaret and Jane O'Malley were still living there and I was fortunate to see that special room. It had a single cot, a small table with the traditional china pitcher and

Shrine of Our Lady of Fatima
It is situated directly west of the front entrance to the church.
Dedicated June 9, 1963.

bowl, a straight-backed chair and a crucifix. On the walls
hung pictures of priests who had visited there.

One of the priests who made regular stops at the
O'Malley home was from Sonora. At that time the Indians were many and quite "uncivilized," especially those
living in the mountain areas close to Sonora. Father
O'Connor and other priests learned the hard way to put
all their coats and extra clothing under lock and key
because the zealous missionary from Sonora always
appropriated all he could get for his Indians!

Before St. Patrick's Church was built, the nearest
church was in Stockton. Occasionally a pastor from Stockton came and held services in local homes. But, for the
most part, the sturdy pioneers brought their families on
Sunday to the parish church in Stockton. In the early
1880s a parish was formed at Modesto with St. Patrick's
Mission Church of Atlanta being a part of that parish.
The Reverend P. Walsh was the pastor. When Father
Walsh died, Father McGuire became pastor and remained
so for several years. Then, the position was occupied by
the beloved Father O'Connor under whose direction the
mission church was built. During his tenure as pastor,
the little church was remodeled, adding a new front and
redecorating the interior. Also at this time, the church
building was enlarged as more room was needed. There
was on top of the original church a rather ornate cross
which Father O'Connor had removed when the new front
was added. This cross served to mark the first grave in
the cemetery which was that of Patrick Brennan. It was
indeed a strange sight to passersby to see that cross standing in its solitude amid the barren plains.

Father O'Connor passed away December 26, 1911 and
was succeeded by Father W. E. McGough. During

The original St. Patrick's Church, above,
and after remodeling, below.
(The picture below Courtesy of Margaret & Jane O'Malley)

McGough's administration, more land was donated by Mr. O'Malley for cemetery purposes and improvements. Also the beautiful stained glass windows which adorned the mission church were donated by McGough. They had previously belonged to St. Agnes Chapel in Stockton and had been gifted to that chapel by the pioneers whose names were inscribed thereon.

After World War I, a church was built in Manteca and a new parish formed which included St. Patrick's. Now St. Patrick's was no longer a mission to St. Stanislaus Catholic Church in Modesto, but a mission to St. Anthony's Parish in Manteca. Father John Marchisio was named the first pastor of the new Manteca parish. He too had St. Patrick's mission church painted and new furniture installed during his tenure.

It is worthy of note that through the vicissitudes of time from 1878 to the present, St. Patrick's Church at Atlanta remained free from debt and in good standing. No small credit is due to the pioneers, among them being John B. O'Malley, Michael Carroll, Peter Vinet, Daniel Brennan, Patrick Brennan, Thomas Brennan, Michael McCormack, Lawrence Hearty, John Murphy, Cornelius Lamasney, John Gannan, Michael Donelly, Vincent Brignolo, Laurence Hearty, Denis O'Neil, Patrick Sexton, John Gannon, Esper Due and others.

In the early 1940s a drive was held in the parish to pledge a sum of money for the construction of a new and larger church. The old mission church had been condemned as unsafe and was much too small for the three hundred Catholic families then in the parish. The drive was successful and the new church was started in 1945 under the supervision of Father Dennis Glennon, then pastor of St. Anthony's Parish in Manteca and of St.

Patrick's Mission Church. The Church building itself cost approximately $40,000 and many parishioners made special contributions which included the beautiful and priceless stained glass windows which adorn the church today. The donor's name is inscribed on each window. The church was completed in 1946 and upon its dedication was officially made a parish and is now known as St. Patrick's Parish. The late Father Leon Bernard was appointed as the first pastor of the new parish. The architects were Wilton, Smith & Minton of San Francisco and the building contractor was H. Beuving of Ripon. In 1966, the east wing of the church and the bell tower were constructed. Father James Maloney was pastor at the time. After his untimely death in April 1966, the bell tower was dedicated to him and a bronze plaque was installed in his memory.

In 1950 a new parish, St. Francis of Rome, was formed in Riverbank and a portion of St. Patrick's Parish on the on the south and east side of Escalon was annexed to the new Riverbank parish.

In the 1950s the parish needed a home for its priest. A fine modern home was constructed at a little under $20,000. Soon the parishioners felt they needed a parish hall for the many parish organizations to hold their meetings and also for the young people of the parish to have for their sports and other activities. A parish hall was built in 1951 at a cost of $42,250. A large stage, public address system, large main section for indoor sports and other events and a fully equipped modern kitchen and meeting room were included. Additional land for a parking lot and land to enlarge the cemetery was purchased at this time.

It seems so long ago that Atlanta was a booming com-

The new St. Patrick's Church built in 1946.
To the left are the rectory and the classrooms.

munity. Today we face the reality that only two landmarks remain. The building which housed the Methodist Church (1878) is still standing today at its original location, and St. Patrick's Church is at same location as in 1878. The original mission erected along the west side of Hearty Road (now known as Carrolton Road) was eliminated in 1946 when the present structure was built on that same location.

MUSIC IN THE CHURCH

In the mission church was a pump organ which was

Fr. Louis L. Sweeny stands beside the original pump organ which John B. O'Malley gave to the church in 1878. The photograph was taken during the church's centennial in 1978.

donated by the O'Malley family. Mr. O'Malley purchased it in San Francisco in 1868 for $1000. This same organ was installed in the new church built in 1946 and used for several years. In 1954 a drive to purchase an electric organ was spearheaded by some of the church's choir members. With success attained, a new electric organ was purchased the same year for $3000 from Reynolds Piano Co. in Modesto. A number of years later, the Young Ladies Institute, a Catholic women's group, purchased an electric organ in memory of one of its members who had died at a young age. Still later, another electric organ was donated. In 1998 a new Leslie electronic organ was donated by Mary Pope Eichoff, who is a charter member of the Young Ladies Institute and a long-time parishioner of St. Patrick's Church. The organ is a Protégé model Allen organ from the Allen Organ Company. Together with the sound system it cost $29,317. An adult choir has been formed and usually they sing for special holy days accompanied by that organ.

The first organist in the Mission Church of St. Patrick was Margaret O'Malley. In subsequent years Faye Swass Medeiros, Evelyn Lucas Cellini, Lucille Carvalho Solaegui, and Amanda Rodoani also played the "pump" organ in the old mission church. Names of some of the organists who provided music in the present church include Ernest Azevedo, Catherine Christensen Stewart, Norma Franzia Roig, Mary Helen Aloisio, Cynthia Alfieri, Charles Rossi, David Vieira. The present church organist is Madeline Archibeque.

The Diocese of Stockton

In February 1962, Pope John XXIII divided the Archdiocese of San Francisco, of which St. Patrick's Parish had always been a part. From that point to the present, St. Patrick's Parish is included in the Diocese of Stockton. Bishop Hugh A. Donohue, D.D. Ph.D., was the first Bishop of Stockton. He was Auxiliary Bishop of San Francisco. Bishop Donohue was born in 1905 in San Francisco and ordained June 1930. He was appointed Auxiliary Bishop of San Francisco in August, 1947.

The headquarters for the new Diocese of Stockton are at the Church of the Annunciation, which is now known as the Cathedral of the Annunciation. Included in the Diocese of Stockton are San Joaquin, Stanislaus, Tuolumne, Mono, Alpine and Calaveras counties. All these changes came about after the death of Archbishop

John J. Mitty of San Francisco. The Pope appointed
Bishop Joseph T. McGucken of Sacramento as the new
Archbishop of the Diocese of San Francisco. The population increase in the area warranted the establishment
of a separate diocese for all the counties mentioned above.

THE PAINTING OF SAINT PATRICK

You will see hanging on the wall near the altar of St.
Patrick's Church a very old painting of St. Patrick. This
painting hung over the altar of the old mission church
before the year 1900 and up to the time the old edifice
was demolished. Then, for a long time, it hung on an
easel in a corner of the loft of the new church and had
been severely vandalized. In 1981, I had it restored by
artist Oscar Galgiani of Stockton. It remains in its original frame today. When the artist took the frame apart,
he found that it had been assembled with square nails.
There is no indication of the name of the artist who
painted this lovely work, nor is there a date. However,
we believe that the painting is well over one hundred years
old. Some of us just like to believe that St. Patrick himself had a hand in putting it in a place where it would be
well kept and appreciated—here at St. Patrick's Church.

STATUES IN THE CHURCH

Most of the statues in the church today are of historical
value. The statue of St. Theresa was given to St. Patrick's
by Mrs. Vincent (Lena) Osterero, the statue of St. Anne
was donated by Anne Swass, the statue of St. Anthony
was donated by Mr. and Mrs. John Murphy (pioneers),
the statue of St. Joseph was donated by the O'Malley Family (pioneers), the statue of the Blessed Virgin Mary was
donated by Mr. & Mrs. Manuel Carvalho, the statue of

SAINT PATRICK

This oil-on-linen painting originally hung over the altar of St. Patrick's Mission Church from 1878 to about 1925. The artist is unknown. The Mission Church stood directly east of this present church building. The painting was restored in 1981, thus maintaining its historical value for future generations. At the time the Mission Church was built in 1878, there were predominantly Irish settlers in this, the Atlanta District. These people gave the honor of St. Patrick's name to their place of worship in the New Land of America.

March 17, 1984

Queen Isabella was donated by the Ripon Portuguese Society. In 1988, the Our Lady of Fatima statue in the church was donated by Alerd and Georgiana Caton. Father James O'Dwyer went to the Azores to purchase it for them. The statue of St. Patrick was donated by Tony and Carol Lawrence, Frank and Bernadette Machado and Pete and Cora Vander Werff.

The statues of St. Theresa, St. Anne, St. Anthony, St. Joseph and the Blessed Virgin Mary were in the church already in the early 1900s. The others came after 1940.

Parish Clubs & Organizations

The "Our Lady of Fatima Celebration" club was organized July 20, 1986. Present were Frank V. Borba, Frank Machado, Tony and Evelyn Luis, Mrs. Dorothy Teixeira, Manuel Borba, Alerd Caton, Joe Sousa, Joe and Elsie Cunha, Tony Rocha Jr., Luiz Barcelos, Durvalho Gomes and Father James O'Dwyer. Those chosen for first officers were President, Frank V. Borba; Vice-President, Frank Machado; Secretary, Dorothy Teixeira; Treasurer, Catherine Rocha; and Marshall, Tony Luis. Every year on Labor Day weekend, a celebration is held in honor of Our Lady of Fatima and a Mass and procession precede the free lunch which is served to everyone attending. In the afternoon, an auction is held of donated items which, among other items, include dairy cows, Portuguese breads, handmade items, needlework, etc. In the evening, a bullfight is held at Frank V. Borba Arena north of Escalon.

The "Our Lady of Fatima Celebration" club has contributed a great deal to St. Patrick's Church and parish. Some of their projects have included blacktopping the parking lot west of the parish hall, and in 1988 they built eight classrooms behind the parish hall and added new restrooms at a cost of $173,243. New equipment for the kitchen was purchased and the whole kitchen remodeled. Additionally, a patio was added to the west side of the parish hall. Six additional classrooms for the Confraternity of Christian Doctrine (C.C.D.) were built in 1992 on the east side of the existing eight classrooms, at a cost of $76,866.

On the west end of the parish hall was built the "Our Lady of Fatima Chapel" along with a storage room and new restrooms for the hall in 1993. Five stained glass windows for the chapel were purchased and donated by five couples who are members of St. Patrick's Parish. The Tabernacle in the Chapel was purchased and donated by Father James O'Dwyer in memory of his father.

The "Our Lady of Fatima Celebration" club continues to help with projects to repair, rebuild and maintain the buildings and grounds for the parish.

Young Ladies Institute (YLI)

This Catholic ladies' group has its headquarters in San Francisco and has institutes all over the west coast and Hawaii. The local chapter is called "Our Lady of Fatima" YLI #179 and was started on April 27, 1947 with thirty-nine charter members. Father John Walsh was the first Chaplain. The objectives of this organization are to instill true Catholic ideals and spirit in affairs of church and country, and to foster the moral, mental and social advancement of its members. The YLI supports the education of men to the priesthood through a fund, "The Golden Jubilee Burse." They support the C.C.D. and assist worthy service groups. In 1997, the ladies celebrated the 50th anniversary of YLI #179. A perpetual novena by all members has been ongoing for many years and continues now without fail.

OTHER PARISH ORGANIZATIONS

The parish is proud of its Altar Society. The members decorate the altar for Sunday masses and they also adorn the altar and church for special holidays including Christmas and Easter.

St. Vincent de Paul Society assists the needy of St. Patrick's Parish and the community at large throughout the year. The members also distribute food to needy families at Christmas and Easter time.

The Hispanic Charismatic Community of Evangelization is a prayer group. They attend St. Patrick's and sometimes mass is said at the old Methodist Church (see Methodist Episcopal Church).

For the first time in the history of St. Patrick's, a parish directory was put out in the year 2000. Almost all the parishioners had their pictures taken for this directory. The current pastor, Father Mark Wagner, was in charge. The parish of St. Patrick includes three towns: Escalon, Farmington, and Ripon.

PARISH ADDRESS CHANGES

From the year 1878 through 1915, the address for St. Patrick's Church was—Atlanta, California. Beginning in 1916 to 1995, its address was Escalon, California. In 1995, when Fr. James O' Dwyer was here, he had the address changed to Ripon, California.

However, the church established in 1878 has never moved from its historic location!

REFLECTION

I like what Father Louis L. Sweeny wrote for St. Patrick's Church Centennial in 1978:

> *We try to visualize a little white church near a watering trough at the edge of a wheat field. St. Patrick's Church, 1878. Someone cared enough to put it there. It would know the eager step of the bride, the heavy step of the mourner. It would channel a hundred thousand petitions to God. It would echo the commands of Mt. Sinai and it would catch the whisper of the mercy of God.*

—from the booklet "100th Anniversary, St. Patrick's Church & St. John's Cemetery"

The O'Malley home, built in the late 1860s.
This is the front view before it was razed, taken about 1977.

The John B. O'Malley Family

I would be remiss in capturing an important part of the local history if the story of John B. O'Malley were not remembered. He was a successful, honored and highly respected citizen of San Joaquin County. The life of this good man was excellently portrayed by his labors. His business career was successfully managed, gaining him prosperity and honor that won him the unqualified confidence of all with whom he came in contact. He was born in 1830 in County Roscommon, Ireland. At the age of seventeen, he migrated to America together with his mother, his sister Margaret and his brother, Martin. The ocean voyage took six weeks during which they encountered very stormy weather. Upon landing in this country, they settled in Norwich, Connecticut. In 1849, he married an Irish girl, Miss Ann E. Brennan, who migrated from Ireland and had been well educated in a private school there.

Mr. O'Malley found employment until 1853 on the S.S. *Commonwealth*, a passenger steamer plying between Norwich and New York. The news of the discovery of gold in California was exciting, so he left his family in the east and set out to seek his fortune in the west. Arriv-

ing in San Francisco by way of Panama, he went directly
to Stockton and found work at the Weber House, a lead-
ing hotel of that period, and held the position of manager for four years. Meanwhile, he sent for his wife and
two children and the family resided in Stockton until
1862.

O'Malley did have his turn at mining in the copper
mines near Copperopolis with some men from Stockton,
among them Michael Carroll, who later became his neighbor and lifelong friend. In 1862, Mr. O'Malley purchased
four hundred acres of land seventeen miles southeast of
Stockton on the French Camp Road where he built a
cabin for his family. They lived there until he was able
to complete a large two-story residence. The original cabin
was converted to a blacksmith shop after the family
moved into the new home.

In order to have a good neighbor, Mr. O'Malley sold
half of his original purchase to his friend, Michael Carroll. These two men worked together to make their part
of the county a desirable place in which to live. Eventually, O'Malley owned thirteen hundred acres of good
land. He was a very successful grain farmer and cattle
raiser. A philanthropist in the truest sense, O'Malley
helped a man to be himself and was always ready to lend
a helping hand to those less fortunate. Likewise, he was
a devoted husband and father. In 1899, Mr. & Mrs. John
B. O'Malley celebrated their golden wedding anniversary
at their home surrounded by their children, grandchil-
dren, relatives and friends. They were presented with a
"Gold Brick" which was a special old fashioned brick covered with a gold colored metal and outfitted with a secret
drawer complete with lock and key. The drawer had been
filled with gold coins by the many well-wishers!

Mr. O'Malley died September 26, 1909. His funeral mass was held at St. Mary's Catholic Church in Stockton and twelve Roman Catholic priests joined in the memorial. A throng of laity bore evidence of his popularity among citizens at large. Old friends carried his remains to Atlanta's St. Patrick's Church where he was buried in the cemetery which, in tribute, was named St. John's Catholic Cemetery. On June 29, 1921, Mrs. O'Malley celebrated her ninetieth birthday and many friends and relatives were there to celebrate. She died September 10, 1921, and was laid to rest next to her late husband.

At the time of his death, Mr. O'Malley was the oldest naturalized citizen in the County of San Joaquin, having received his citizenship papers in 1852.

I remember some of the older folks talking about the O'Malleys and referring to John B. O'Malley as "Bishop John." They also told me that he was well known to every priest of that time. Many of them enjoyed his hospitality when traveling in the area.

History is the witness that testifies to the passing of time; it illuminates reality, vitalizes memory, provides guidance in daily life, and brings us tidings of antiquity.

-Marcus T. Cicero

Saint John's Catholic Cemetery

In 1878, the cemetery at St. Patrick's Church of Atlanta came into being with the burial of Patrick Brennan (see St. Patrick's Church). When John B. O'Malley donated the land for the church, he also donated land for the cemetery. The cemetery is contiguous to the north side with St. Patrick's Church, the rectory, and the parish hall on the south side. Over the years, the O'Malley family gave additional land to expand the cemetery. The early day section of the cemetery is referred to as the Pioneer section. Many of the tombstones bear names of Irish immigrants who were a major nationality of the settlers in the Atlanta District. There were no walls or fences around those hallowed grounds. However, some families would build wood fences around their deceased loved one's grave to discourage coyote and other animals from foraging. Families were responsible for keeping the graves of their families free of weeds. Sometimes, the priest would be seen out there with a rake and hoe, cleaning up some forgotten sites.

I spent many Sundays reading the names and admiring the imposing tombstones. One of the plots that

intrigued me was the O'Malley plot. There was a huge olive tree in the middle and on each end of the plot stood glassed-in cases as wide as the plot. Statuettes of favorite saints and other religious articles were kept in those glass cases. The small vases were sometimes filled with small flowers by family. Somewhere between 1936 and 1940 the tree was removed and the glass enclosed cases disappeared together with their contents. One other striking grave stone is that of Vincent Brignole. It is of polished red marble and came by ship from Italy more than one hundred years ago. It still looks brand new. For years, no one seemed to know who was buried in the small plot in the children's section which had a wrought-iron fence around it and no identification. Discovered records show that three little children ages five years to nine months died as a result of a house fire in Escalon and all three are buried in that little plot.

For 105 years the cemetery belonged to St. Patrick's Church. William J. Murphy kept cemetery records and assigned plots for many years before 1941. In those early years, one had to be a resident of the Atlanta District and a church-going member of St. Patrick's Church to be given the right to be buried in St. John's Cemetery. Now, generally, any Catholic may be buried there. In 1983, the cemetery came under the jurisdiction of the new Diocese of Stockton. The first manager of the cemetery, Mrs. Eve-

Early day grave in St. John's Cemetery.

Veterans' Memorial.
Photo courtesy of
Lorraine Vasconcellos.

lyn Swass, was appointed by Reverend Monsignor James C. Cain, Vicar General of the Diocese of Stockton. Mrs. Swass retired in 1997 after fourteen years in that position. However, she substitutes occasionally for the new manager, Cyndy Rodriguez.

Under Mrs. Swass' direction, many improvements took place. Grave sites were prepared with pre-installed cement liners and a name designation was given to each new section: Mother Cabrini, St. Isabel, and Our Lady of Guadalupe sections. In the Our Lady of Guadalupe section, all graves have double depth liners. Some people do not like the double depth sections as their future plans are to have themselves at rest side by side with their mate.

There is a section set aside for Cremains and also a small area for indigents at the northwest end of the Pioneer section. Then there are two sections with no liners—East Lawn and West Lawn. Also, extensive reconstruction has been carried out on the baby section in the Pioneer area.

In the Mother Cabrini section, a new flag pole has been erected on the mound and dedicated "In Memory of all Military Veterans, both Men and Women—Year 2000." The area is nicely landscaped and designed to hold military memorials on special days. Two memorial granite benches have been installed. One is a memorial to Thomas and Alice Corey, and the other is a memorial to Mr. and Mrs. Manuel S. Blanco and family. The Knights of Columbus initiated and completed the installation of a granite marker, "In Memory of Unborn Children" in this same section.

In 1966, a 104-crypt mausoleum was built on the west side of the cemetery. Due to need, two new sections were added in 1971. In the year 2000, the Diocese of Stockton embarked on Phase I of a new and bigger mausoleum. When Phase II of this project is implemented, a chapel will be added. There will also be spaces in the new mausoleum for Cremains. The builders of this project are Oliver & Co., Richmond, California. Presently, Monsignor Cain is the Director of Cemeteries for the Diocese.

Over all the years, only one priest has been buried in St. John's Cemetery—the beloved Father James Maloney, who died suddenly while driving his car in the Bay Area in 1966. The *Escalon Times* wrote a tribute to him which reads "Escalon lost one of its staunchest supporters last week with the passing of Father James Maloney, pastor of St. Patrick's Church. Father Maloney just loved everyone and everyone just loved him. He had a keen

Sketch of new Mausoleum by Mark Swass.

wit, a lovely philosophy of life, was gracious and felt a deep kinship with his fellowmen. He was only with us for about 7 years but in that scant period of time, he made a host of friends. Father Maloney loved his parish so much that he chose to remain with it always and is the first priest to be buried in St. John's Cemetery in its long and memorable history." Further stated was the knowledge that other priests would come to carry on, but to the writer of the *Escalon Times* article, "the bright social hall, manse and graceful church and towering spire will always be a memorial to Father James Maloney because its cheerfulness is a reflection of his life on earth." Father Louis L. Sweeny came to take Father Maloney's place in 1966 and remained until September 1, 1981, when he was transferred to St. Joachim's Church in Newman. Father James O'Dwyer was his replacement and he remained until 1983 when he left for Ireland. During his absence, Father Cornelius DeGroot was appointed to fill in. In September of 1985, Father O'Dwyer returned from Ireland and resumed his position at St. Patrick's Church. He remained until 1997 and was replaced by Father Mark Wagner, who is the parish priest at this writing.

Today, the cemetery has a groundskeeper/grave digger—Bob Freeseha, who has worked at this cemetery for twenty years. He is in charge of the upkeep of the cemetery and also of opening and closing the graves for funerals.

The brick wall on the east and south sides of the cemetery was built by Henry Grube, master bricklayer and builder. The bricks were donated by Giuseppe Franzia, founder of the Franzia Winery.

On the south end of the cemetery, near the church, an arbor was built where a big old Cedar tree once stood, the victim of a winter storm. In 1998, four commemorative granite benches and a statue of St. Francis were installed in the arbor which is surrounded by Maple and Podocarpus trees. The Statue of St. Francis enhances the Franzia crypts on the east side of the church. The benches are memorials as follows: In Memory of Irma Simoni, by her husband Gil; In Memory of the Baciocco and Giuntoli Families, by Reno and Reanna Giuntoli; In Memory of Our Betti and Swass Loved Ones, by Mark and Evelyn Swass Family; In Memory of the Garibaldi, Persano, and Alfieri Families, by Elsie Alfieri.

Near the south end of the Pioneer section of the cemetery are the family plots of O'Malley, Brennan, Cosgriff, Carroll, Brignole, Murphy, Vinet, Lamasney, Due and

other pioneers. On the monument marking the grave of
the Marcy family is this inscription:

> Pause, stranger, as you pass by,
> As you are now, so once was I.
> As I am now, soon you will be,
> Reflect on death, and pray for me.

The Van Allen School

In the early days of San Joaquin County, there were six school districts. One was the New Hope District which covered a large area in the southeasterly section of the county. Part of that area was to become the Van Allen School District. In the year 1860, a petition was presented to the Board of Supervisors of San Joaquin County by Isop Watson and other citizens for the formation of a new school district in this large area. There being no objections, the Board of Supervisors granted that as much of the Congressional Township Number 2 South, Range Nine East, Mount Diablo Base and Meridian as lies in San Joaquin County should constitute a new district to be known as the Stanislaus School District. On November 29, 1860, another petition was presented to the Board of Supervisors of San Joaquin County by Patrick Brennan and others of this section, naming the boundaries and description of certain lands to form a new district, and naming it Zinc House School District. The petition was granted. The school house was located on Earnest Wagoner's land, which today may be identified as being the parcel of land which is situated at the southwest corner of the intersection of Yosemite Avenue (formerly French Camp Road and now State Highway 120) and Wagner Road (see Atlanta School).

September 30, 1861 was a great day for the Van Allen School District because it was on this day that a pioneer of the area, Christopher von Glahn and others in this vicinity presented to the Board of Supervisors of San Joaquin County, their petition for the formation of a new school district. The petition was granted and the district was named Van Allen after the man who was, at the time, County Superintendent of Schools. At first, the Van Allen School was on the northwest side of Van Allen Road and French Camp Road. Patrick Brennan, the property owner, had given permission for the school to be built on his property. In the early days of the Van Allen School District, a problem arose of how to expand to accommodate the growing population. The first school house was a very small one-room structure and more room was needed. The present site of Van Allen School was at one time part of the John B. O'Malley holdings, but fell into the hands of Lukey Brennan, a brother of Mrs. John B. O'Malley, and, eventually came under ownership of Mr. A. W. Hunsucker of Atlanta, California. Mr. Hunsucker deeded to the Van Allen School District one acre of land on the 8th day of March 1873 for the sum of One Dollar in GOLD! After the turn of the century, Mr. R. B. Teefy, then President of the San Joaquin Valley Bank, who had since acquired the land adjoining the school property, donated an additional two acres of land east of and adjacent to the original site for a school yard and playground. Then, the one-room structure on the west side of the road was uprooted and moved to John Brennan's place where it was used as a barn for a number of years before finally being razed. The land reverted back to Patrick Brennan. At once, a new and larger one-room school house was constructed on the new site, the men

The Van Allen School built in 1913. The author
graduated from this school in 1936.

of the district pitching in with the building. At one time,
school enrollment reached seventy students. For the year
ending June 30, 1878, the Van Allen School showed a
total enrollment of fifty-six students of which twenty-nine
were boys and twenty-seven were girls and of this total,
sixteen of them were under five years of age. At that time,
there was one male teacher for all the eight grades and
his monthly salary was $85. Reports show that the school
operated on $100 per month. Mr. John B. O'Malley was
clerk of the Board and the first trustees of the Van Allen

School were: John B. O'Malley, Christopher von Glahn, and Patrick Brennan.

In 1868 an application was presented to the Board of Supervisors by J. Lowery to organize a new school district which would embrace a part of the Van Allen School District. The petition was granted and the new district was named the Lone Tree School District. However, in the early 1900s many of the landowners lost their farms or moved off the land and the Lone Tree School District lapsed. After the Oakdale Irrigation District was organized and canals were built to carry water to the land during the years 1912 to the 1960s, people came back to the land and the Lone Tree School District sprang back to life. However, that school district no longer exists.

The Van Allen School District made great progress and as more families moved into the area, the schoolhouse was no longer adequate. On November 15, 1912 a public meeting was held in the school house for the purpose of considering the feasibility of bonding the district to build a new modern school house to accommodate the increase in the number of students. It was agreed by the taxpayers present to instruct the trustees to call an election for the purpose of obtaining funds to build a new schoolhouse and to employ the necessary professional services. Stone and Wright of Stockton were the architects. On June 27, 1913 an election was held and the bonds were approved for $8000 to construct and equip a new schoolhouse. The contract was awarded to the lowest bidder, C. C. Busch, who bid $5924. Upon completion a gala dedication was held October 25, 1913. During the celebration Mr. James P. Carroll, a prominent farmer of this section and one of the first pupils of the school, told a very interesting version of the history of the Van Allen School district from its formation in 1861 and told of the many other districts which had been formed from this one. Mrs. John B. O'Malley who had been a resident of the community for the past fifty-two years, voiced her congratulations to those who were instrumental in making the district what it is. She had seen three schoolhouses built for the Van Allen School. In the early 1950s the two story schoolhouse was razed and the present structure we see today was built by C. T. Brayton & Sons of Escalon. It was ready for occupancy in March 1953. Interestingly, the slate blackboards were saved from the old school and installed in this new one.

The Van Allen School has produced many fine citizens, and its basic teachings have been the foundation for the future success of many of its graduates.

In 1967, the Van Allen School District became a part of the Escalon Unified School District. The class of 1971 was the last eighth grade class to graduate from Van Allen School. El Portal Middle School had opened in Escalon and all 7th and 8th grade students attended there.

Van Allen has been designated the school of growth in the Escalon Unified School District. In the spring of 1996 and 1997 six acres of new playground were added to the Van Allen site. Additional portable classrooms were added to accommodate the growth of the population in the area.

History balances the frustration of "how far we have to go" with satisfaction of "how far we have come." It teaches us tolerance for the human shortcoming and imperfections which are not uniquely of our generation, but of all time.

-Lewis F. Powell Jr.

Escalon

Escalon, at the far southeasterly corner of San Joaquin County, was non-existent when the town of Atlanta was flourishing. John Wheeler Jones (1821-1893), settled out on the barren plain in 1855. It was a dry God-forsaken country when he arrived. He planted the first wheat ever planted in this area. He became a big grain grower as the years went along. Jones owned considerable land in the Atlanta area. His holdings included 8000 acres in the Escalon vicinity, 2500 acres of grazing land on the west side of San Joaquin County, 25,000 acres in neighboring Stanislaus County and 8000 acres in Tulare County. When he first arrived, there were squatters nearby and he rousted them. He also bought out the "Blue Tent Tavern" on the north side of what is now State Highway 120, about 1 ¼ miles east of where Escalon is today. Some folks can identify it closer as being the Wilson Ranch. The tavern was so named because of the color of the tent which housed the tavern.

In the 1850s, homes were miles apart and roads were only rutted wagon trails. Travel was by horseback or by horse and buggy. A trip to Stockton for supplies was either a one–day event, or a three– or four–day trip depending on the weather. Slowly, some of the businesses that set up in Escalon were a livery stable, blacksmith shop, and horse-shoeing establishment, and, of course, a bar—Jackson's Bar.

Mr. Jones built a two story brick home in 1867 at a cost of $12,000. The bricks were made from clay which lay in a field about three hundred yards east of Sexton Road on the Tidewater Railroad line. The walls of the home were from twelve to fourteen inches thick with an air space in the middle of the wall from top to bottom. It became a stopping place for many prospectors who were on their way to the gold mines. The home was then referred to as "The Mansion of the Prairie." The last remaining daughter, Miss Alice D. Jones, lived there. I knew her in the early 1940s and she was a stately, tall woman who still wore those lovely garments from long ago. Miss Jones was a person of great generosity and the community benefited in many ways. She gave the newly founded Escalon Union High School District the use of this brick home for the first high school building in the community (1919-1922). Later she gave the building to Dr. von Hungen for a community hospital. Incidentally, this was not the first hospital in Escalon. The first one was established in the second story of the home of Mrs. Mae Arrington at St. Clair and Sacramento streets. That building is still standing and that second story still has the sinks from that era hanging on the wall. Dr. Benson was the local physician at that time and he delivered many of the local babies born there including Marcelle Widman, daughter of Otto and Florence Widman, long time area dairy farmers.

Today the Jones Mansion is privately owned and has been restored to its regal stature.

When Mr. Jones died in 1893, he deeded the home and surrounding property to his son, James. Immediately,

James Jones had the area surveyed and lots laid out. In 1895, he also granted the right-of-way for the railroad to the Claus Spreckels Railway which became the Atchison, Topeka and Santa Fe Railroad. Today, it is called the Burlington-Northern-Santa Fe Railroad. All the area which James Jones had surveyed was sold to J. W. Coley who got the village of Escalon started. Mr. Frank Thornton who knew all these people, told me that when Coley purchased the surveyed area he did not want to use someone else's idea, so he re-surveyed it and laid it out on a diagonal the way the railroad tracks went.

The whole Main Street of the town burned down in the big fire of 1920. There have been subsequent destructive fires in and around the town but none as serious as the 1920 fire.

THE BURWOOD-ESCALON AREA

This area was studded with oak trees. The largest forest of oak trees was known as Huntley's Grove. In the very late 1800s and the beginning of the 1900s when people started to arrive, they cut down many of the oak trees to use for firewood for cooking and heating. Thus a great many of the trees were cut down, but this procedure stopped when the trains started coming through Escalon carrying coal which was then used in place of the wood. Today there are few oak trees left, partially due to the clearing of the land for orchards, vineyards, dairies, and homes. One very large oak tree still lives on the land that once was Burwood School on River Road.

THE MOLL RANCH

At the turn of the twentieth century, many people were migrating to California from all over the world. One was a retired sea captain who purchased a fifteen acre parcel about 1 ½ miles west of the settlement of Escalon, on French Camp Road. This sea captain built a very tall windmill and tank house in the shape of a lighthouse on his property. It was reinforced with six-inch by six-inch redwood timbers and the one thousand gallon water tank at the very top was also of redwood. His property was known as the Moll Ranch and that name stuck for identification purposes. Mrs. Lura Morgenson Casto, well-known local piano teacher and accompanist for silent movies, lived on that ranch with her husband when they moved to California. In the short while they were there, a baby girl was born to them and also died. They buried the infant under a massive apricot tree which stood alone at the easterly end of the property. Given its size, the tree had to be at least sixty years old at that time. One can imagine a traveler dropping an apricot pit on his travels—or it fell out of his saddle bag. That tree was cut down about 1955. I grew up on the Moll Ranch.

The Covell Ranch

About two miles west of Escalon was the electric train stop known as Volstead. The land at that location was owned by George Covell of the Hotel Covell in Modesto, California. The Covells donated the money for Covell College, part of the University of the Pacific, in Stockton, California.

Tidewater Southern Railway

The Tidewater Southern Railway (T.S.Ry) started out as an interurban electric railway. It was to run from Stockton, California, down the San Joaquin Valley south to Fresno. The T.S.Ry was incorporated to build a standard gauge railroad from Stockton south in 1910. By 1910 the silt had built up to a point that it forced back river navigation on the San Joaquin River to Stockton. Earlier, boats could navigate all the way to Fresno from Stockton. Hence, the name "Tidewater" was fitting. In 1912, the Tidewater & Southern Transit Company consolidated with the railroad and formed the Tidewater Southern Railway.

In 1912, a stretch of electric railway was opened from Stockton to Modesto for a distance of thirty-three miles. The first equipment consisted of a home-made wooden steeple-cab electric locomotive which was built on a flat car. Three Jewett-built cars were the first passenger equipment on this little railway. Tidewater Southern was operating twenty-four trains daily between Stockton and Modesto. The thirty-three-mile trip took sixty-five minutes. Picnic trains were run to the Stanislaus River during nice weather. This line went through Atlanta and Escalon and made many stops along the way to pick up folks along the line.

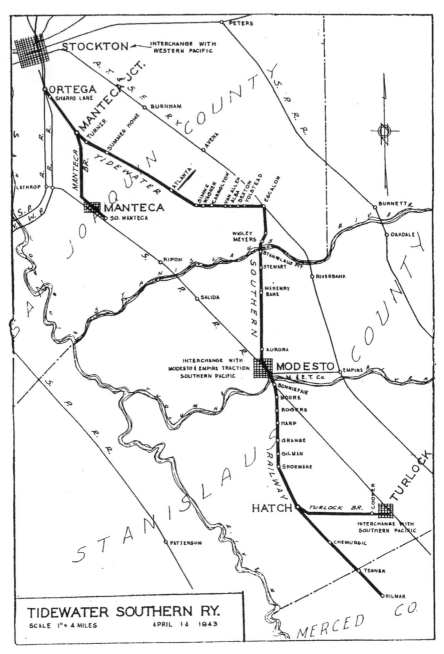

Route of the Tidewater Southern Railway
through the Atlanta District

The southward extension of the rail line dovetailed into plans of the Western Pacific Railroad and a majority of stock was purchased in 1917 by Western Pacific of the Tidewater Southern Railroad. Now T.S.Ry was under new ownership. This brought many changes, including the purchase of steam locomotives. As time went on, freight traffic was increasing and passenger traffic was decreasing due to the use of automobiles. The last interurban electric train ran on May 26, 1932. Some of the coaches were de-motored and used as section houses.

When I was a kid, the electric passenger trains ran by our house. They were referred to as "old slow, tired and easy." I think it was because the trains never picked up speed but chugged along at a comfortable "click-clack" down the tracks. Folks who live in the vicinity of the railroad tracks still use that phrase to describe the freight trains traveling up and down the rails today.

History is a cyclic poem written by Time
Upon the memories of man.
                              -Percy Bysshe Shelley

Dent Township

(The following information is courtesy of the U.S. Depart-ment of the Interior, General Land Office.)
The initial point of the Mount Diablo Meridian was established on Friday, July 18, 1851 by Leander Ransome, Deputy Surveyor at the time, under instructions issued July 8, 1851, by Samuel D. King, Esquire, Surveyor General of California at San Francisco, California. A marker has been placed on the summit of Mount Diablo at 3,849 feet elevation, establishing the East-West base line and North-South Meridian. Today, when a description of a piece of land is made by a surveyor, all those lines and that description are from the Mount Diablo Base and Meridian.

Soon after California was admitted to the Union in 1850, the surveyors came out to divide the state into townships and sections. The Board of Supervisors, in defining the boundaries of three townships created by them, gave no attention to the township area designated by the government surveyors. The believed that it wasn't necessary to limit a township to six square miles. At the time, there were two or three homes in the whole township.

Dent Township was created by the Board of Supervisors on February 17, 1859. It was named after George W. Dent, a resident of Knights Ferry. The newly established township covered a great amount of land which included Knights Ferry within its borders.

The State Legislature sliced Dent Township in half in the year 1860 and formed other townships. That way, all the land which Dent Township covered in Stanislaus County, including Knights Ferry, was passed over to Stanislaus County. The excess land in San Joaquin County was divided into surrounding townships. The boundaries of Dent Township were reestablished in 1864. About 1914, a committee of men from the Escalon settlement journeyed to Ripon and met with some of the local citizens there and agreed to divide Dent Township into an eastern part to be known as Dent Township, and a western part to be named Ripon Township. This move led to the appointment of a Constable for Escalon and a Justice of the Peace also. The constable was Al F. Landon, a very colorful personality. He went everywhere on his horse. It was a common sight to see him ride on his horse into the local bar and order up a drink and have it served to him without getting down off his horse!

Thanks

I feel that I must acknowledge those who have helped in various ways. To those who have passed on—Margaret and Jane O'Malley, John Brennan, members of the Carroll family — I owe a debt of gratitude for the significant information on Atlanta and on St. Patrick's Church which they gave me many years ago. Also a posthumous word of thanks to a well-liked priest in the parish, Father James Maloney, who provided encouragement and information to include in my writing. Thanks also to my friends, Evelyn Swass for her extensive information about St. John's Cemetery, and Lucy Azevedo for her enthusiastic research on various issues. Very special thanks to my daughter, Cynthia Alfieri who has been a pillar of inspiration and help.

Index